Martin & T.J.'s
Race Car Repair

By Susan Kelly Hearn

Illustrations by Gary Robinson

For additional information contact the publishers:

Lew Boyd
Coastal 181
29 Water Street
Newburyport, MA 01950

Jim Rigney
Rigney Motorsports
54 Wall Street
Wellesley Hills, MA 02481

Copyright © 2003 by Susan Kelly Hearn (story) and Gary Robinson (art).

ISBN: 0-9709854-4-4

First printing, March 2003. Printed in the United States of America.

Dedicated to...

My Mom   *Thanks for the creativity.*
Brooke & Tyler   *Thanks for the inspiration.*
And the support of crew members everywhere.

S.K.H.

For Chris.

G.R.

Martin and T.J. were two mice living in the attic
over a race car shop.

Every day they would squeeze through a tiny hole they found and sneak down behind the wall.

They landed under the race team's workbench. From there they could secretly see all of the tools and equipment, the shiny race cars, and the crew that worked on the cars.

Studying over the cars and listening to the crew, Martin and T.J. soon knew those race cars inside and out.

Early one morning, while watching the crew, the mice heard a strange noise.

CLINK,

CLANK,

CLINK.

"Look out!" cried T.J.
A bolt had fallen out of the front end of the race car. It went rolling and stopped only inches away from Martin and T.J.

8

"Let's get out of here," said Martin. "Hurry before someone sees us."

When they heard the team leave for the races the next morning, Martin and T.J. rushed down to the shop.

"Oh no!" said Martin. "The bolt is still here; nobody found it."

"It's no big deal," said T.J. "They probably used a new bolt to replace this one."

"I sure hope you're right," said Martin. "But what if no one noticed the bolt had fallen out and rolled away?"

Martin and T.J. worried about the team all night.

When the team finally returned home, Martin and T.J. were already waiting under the workbench. They knew in a minute by the long grumbling faces that the races had not gone well, not well at all.

"I don't know what happened to this race car," said Ace, the crew chief. "Last week it was perfect and all of a sudden this week it's awful. What do you think, Logan? You're the driver."

"It was bad," said Logan. "The car was all over the track. I couldn't tell what it was going to do next."

But that wasn't the worst part. The next race, the same thing happened. Again, the crew came home all gloomy and upset, wondering what was wrong with their race car.

"Let's all get to work and get this car running like it should," shouted Ace. "Next weekend is our biggest race of the year."

Every day, Martin and T.J. sat only inches away from the missing bolt, hoping and wishing that someone would figure out the problem.

At the end of the week, the team left the shop for the night.

"Well, that's it," said T.J. "They leave tomorrow morning for the biggest race of the season, and they still haven't replaced the missing bolt."

"That's where you and I come in," said Martin. "I've got a plan."

Working together, they dragged the bolt over to the car.

They lifted,

and they shoved,

and they twisted,

and they turned,

working most of the night, until they had the bolt back
in its proper place.

Standing back to check out
their work, Martin noticed he
had accidentally left a greasy
paw print on the car. As he went
back to wipe it away, the garage
door squeaked open, and in came
the crew.

Leaving the small paw print behind, Martin
and T.J. dove under the car.

"Let's go" said Ace. "We need to get this car loaded in
the trailer. We don't want to be late for the races."

"Hurry!" whispered Martin from inside the car. "Climb up here. We have to find a place to hide."

The next thing they knew, the car was loaded in the trailer, and the door was closed behind them.

"It's so dark in here I can't see a thing," said T.J. "Oh no, what's happening now?"

"We're moving," answered Martin. "Hang on tight."

The race car hauler came to a stop and the the crew rolled the car out of the trailer.

Glancing out the window, Martin heard the roar of a racing engine. "Oh boy, we're in big trouble now. We're at the races," he said.

"What should we do?" asked T.J.

"There's nothing we can do but hold on," answered Martin. "If we jump down now, we'll never get back home!"

Logan put on his helmet, fired up the motor, and headed for the race track.

Martin and T.J. held on to the roll cage with all their might.
"Hey, this isn't too bad," yelled T.J. "The car seems to be
running good."

"It's not too bad yet, but this is only warm-ups," Martin
shouted back. "I hope we got that bolt screwed in tight
enough so it doesn't fall out."

"Get a good grip," said Martin. "The big race is about to start." Lap after lap after lap, Logan raced the car around the track. Cars were sliding in all directions, the dust was flying, the crowd was cheering with excitement, and T.J. wasn't feeling very well.

"I don't think I can hold on much longer!" shouted T.J.
Looking up to see the flagger wave the checkered flag,
Martin yelled back, "Don't let go! The race is over!"

The car came to a stop.

"Hooray! Yahoo!" The crowd was yelling and cheering so loud that Martin had to see what was going on.

Peeking out, he said, "T.J., we won the race! We're in victory lane."

T.J. scrambled up to take a look for himself. Bright lights started flashing all around them.

"They're taking pictures." said Martin. "Quick, get back down."

The mice stayed hidden until everything was loaded back in the trailer and the door was closed.

The trailer pulled out of the track to go home. Martin and T.J. climbed down from the car to get a closer look at the great big golden trophy.

"Hey, look at this," said T.J.

"Wow! It's a victory lane picture," said Martin.

"This is great! I can't believe they won the race," said T.J. "But what's this on the front of the car?"

28

"Hey, that's my paw print!" Martin said proudly.
Martin smiled, knowing that big or small, they
were a part of the team.

The race cars in this story are called **Dirt Modifieds**. There are many different types of race cars that race all over the world. Here are just a few of them.

Vintage Stock

Indy Car

Winston Cup Car

Late Model Car

Sprint Car

Quarter Midget

Look carefully at the pictures in this book. Can you
help the team find the tools listed below?

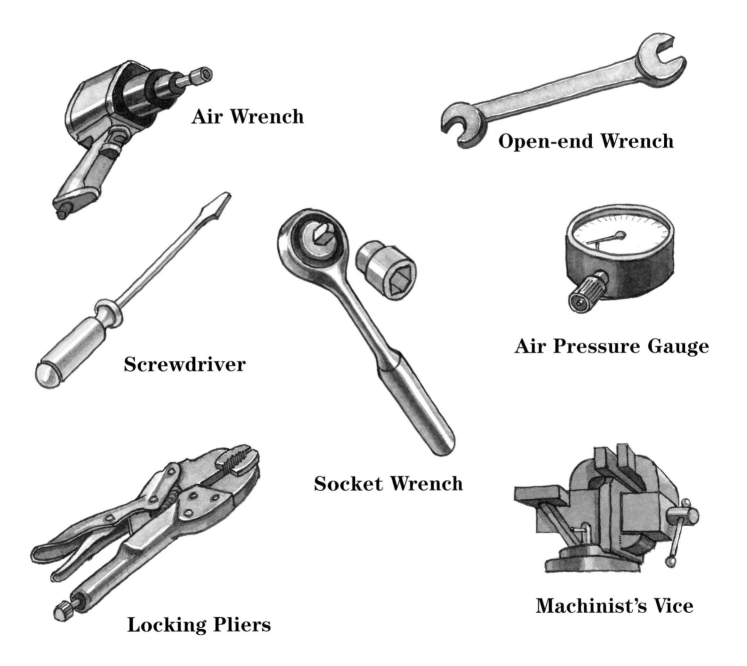

Air Wrench

Open-end Wrench

Screwdriver

Air Pressure Gauge

Socket Wrench

Locking Pliers

Machinist's Vice

About the Author

Susan Kelly Hearn grew up on a farm in Pine Bush, New York. She currently lives in Vernon, New Jersey with her husband, professional race car driver Brett Hearn, and their two children, Brooke and Tyler.

Some of Susan's race team responsibilities include producing the vinyl graphics for the race cars and equipment, managing souvenir sales and fan relations, and organizing charity fund raising activities.

For more information please visit Susan online at *www.bretthearn.com*.

Photo: www.sharpimages.com

About the Illustrator

Gary Robinson is a native of Newburyport, Massachusetts, where he started drawing cartoons on the sidewalks as a small boy. He studied at Massachusetts College of Art and now works as a cartoonist and illustrator. This is his first children's book.

Gary lives in Newburyport with his wife, Chris, and their children, Imogene, Garth, and Rose. He can be reached at *g-c-robinson@worldnet.att.net*

Credits

Jim Rigney   *Editor*
Sandra Rigney   *Design and Art Direction*
Joyce Wells   *Cover Design*
MaryRose Moskell   *Project Coordinator*